The Buddha's Guide to Producing Electronic Music

Table of Contents

Chapter 1. Introduction

In the serene path of sonic exploration, a unique fusion has emerged, entwining the ancient wisdom of Gautama Buddha with the powerful, evocative world of electronic music production. Our Special Report, "The Buddha's Guide to Producing Electronic Music," unravels this harmonious sphere where spirituality breathes life into the digital realm. The Buddha's teachings unfurl with electronic overtones, guiding you to creating not just resonating frequencies but masterpieces that truly touch the soul. Whether you're a seasoned music producer or just embarking on your auditory journey, you'll find this guide enlightening and transformative. Discover the joy of producing electronic music with a sense of calmness, mindfulness, and inner peace. Let's embark together on this enlightening journey of rhythmic harmony and mindful creation.

Chapter 2. The Sound of Silence: An Introduction to Mindful Music Production

There is a profound connection between the world of sound and the realm of silence, and in electronic music production, nothing is more essential than comprehending and honoring this relationship. Yet silence is not merely an absence of sound. From the perspective of mindful music production, it's a living breathing entity.

2.1. Understanding the Sound of Silence

Silence in music is the canvas upon which the notes are painted. Without silence, sound would have no framework, no support, and no meaning. In a spiritual context, silence represents the void, the infinite, the source from which all manifestations arise. Both in music and in Buddhism, silence is not just about the absence of sound - it's about potential.

Imagine a blank canvas not just as an absence of color, but as a space full of potential colors and forms. In the same way, silence in music is potential sound – and understanding this is the key.

The challenge here for those newer to production is embracing the spatial dimensions of silence and the pause it symbolically represents between sounds. In terms of sonic structure, how you space your sounds can bring forth an entirely different emotional response from your listeners, shaping their journey through your creation.

Often, novice producers crammed their tracks full of elements trying to make them sound 'full'. However, this frequently results in a muddied, over-saturated sonic experience. Mastery lies in realizing the potency of silence. 'Less is more' is a mantra that is as fitting as ever in music production.

2.2. Harnessing Silence for Mindful Music Production

Silence is your ally; in fact, it's fundamental to your music production. As you work, carve out space for silence in your compositions. View it not as an enemy or void, but as another instrument at your disposal that you're playing with equal prowess and attention.

Remember, creating electronic music isn't about saturating the soundscape; it's about communicating emotions. How are you supposed to listen if you're always speaking? The same concept applies to music. Carefully consider where you place the beats, synths, and other sound elements, and always leave room for the sound of silence. The careful arrangement of silence within a soundscape is a skill that requires patience and mindfulness to master.

2.3. Reflecting Void in Your Electronic Music Production

In Buddhism, void is the state of mind free from thoughts, emotions, or desires. It symbolizes an absence of worldly disturbance and distractions, the absolute peace. Just like emptiness, silence holds a similar significance in electronic music production.

To reflect the void, you need to equip yourself with the power of mindful listening. Mindful listening is the practice of fully concentrating on the present moment, peacefully acknowledging and accepting your feelings, thoughts, and bodily sensations without any judgment. Train yourself to incorporate mindfulness in your music production, positively influencing not just your creations, but your overall peace of mind.

2.4. Utilizing Mantras in Your Music

In Buddhism, mantras are used as a tool to protect the mind. They are a powerful combination of sounds and vibrations that, when used with intention, can have a transformative impact on the mind. Electronic music producers can harness this concept of mantras to create repetitive beats with an intention that resonates through their compositions.

Mantras can be integrated subtly into the music's underlying structure, adding a rhythmic layer that provides an opportunity for listeners to engage at a deeper level. A well-placed mantra can transform a track from background noise into a spiritual journey for the listener.

Music production, like any act of creation, is as much about the creator as it is about the audience. By incorporating mindfulness into your creative process, you can not only better resonate with your listeners but also experience the joy of creation at a deeper level.

The art of electronic music production is a journey, not a destination. Embrace silence, embody mindfulness, and let your creations be the reflection of the peace within you. Whether you're a seasoned music producer or a beginner in the world of music production, the power of silence can guide you through every beat and rhythm, nudging you with each pause towards a fulfilling and transformative musical endeavor.

Chapter 3. Building Beats with Buddhism: Infusing Spirituality in Music

In the realm of electronic music production, there exists an intoxicating depth that isn't often explored: the fusion of spirituality and sonic performance. For centuries, humans have used music to transcend the mundanity of existence, to connect with something more profound. This union of the spiritual and the sonic is not new, but recent technological innovations have now allowed us to reach greater depths in this enduring quest. Grounded on ancient wisdom and propelled by new-age sound engineering, let's explore the ways in which Buddhism enhances the beats and empowers the soul.

3.1. Understanding the Rhythm of Life

The first step to using Buddhism in music production involves understanding rhythmic principles. The Buddha taught about the Four Noble Truths and the Eightfold Path, both of which are fundamentally about aligning one's life with the rhythm of existence. This rhythm is unique to each individual, influenced by their experiences, their perception of the world, and their internal spiritual state.

When creating beats, tap into these rhythms. Spend time being still and silent, invite in awareness. Use this deep-seated introspection to guide your music production. Instead of working against the pulses of your life, let them inform your creative process. Your tracks can provide soundscapes that evoke these deepest levels of existence, resonating with others in profound ways.

Anchor your creativity within the day-to-day ebb and flow of the world around you and remember, the Buddha taught about the impermanence of all things. Let this knowledge invigorate your music, give each beat a transient life of its own, every note a fleeting moment in time.

3.2. Harmonizing Your Inner Spirit with Sound

Harmony in music production reflects the Buddhist principle of right understanding. It brings balance to sound and silence and strikes a chord with the listener's inner self. This harmonization isn't just an aural experience but rather it illuminates an intimate bond between the soundscape your beats produce and the aura it engenders.

To achieve this, the focus is not just about making 'correct' harmonies but to remain open to 'experimental' harmonies, to the dissonant and surprising sounds that challenge the status quo. Your tracks, like a vibrant Zen garden, should invite listeners to explore myriad emotions, thoughts, and states of consciousness.

3.3. Mindful Sampling: Embracing the Beauty of the Present

Mindfulness is essential to Buddhism. It champions the ability to be fully present and overcome distractions or distortions in our understanding of the world. Mindful Sampling involves using sounds from your environment to add unique, organic elements to your tracks. These sounds can be anything from your breath, to birds singing, to traffic noise.

As you cultivate mindfulness, you come to appreciate these sounds and recognize their musical potential. Your tracks become living, breathing artifacts of your environment, grounding your listeners in the present moment, a beautiful immemorial encapsulation of the 'now.'

3.4. Training the Mind: The Art of Sonic Meditations

The Buddha preached the importance of meditation in achieving enlightenment. In our context, Sonic Meditation can be a powerful tool. It is a practice that involves becoming immersed in the soundscape, losing oneself in the fantastic journey of vibrations, frequencies, and effects that form your track.

Allow your music production process to have meditative qualities. This state of mind creates an environment where your tracks can breathe and grow organically, free from the constraints of overthinking and worrying about perfection. Using a piece of music as a tool to help focus your mind can unlock creative pathways you would never have considered.

3.5. The Path to Enlightenment: Continuous Learning and Improvement

Finally, Buddhism teaches about continuous learning and improvement - a journey that stretches out indefinitely. Your music production skills will grow and mature over time, just as your spiritual journey will. Embrace new technologies, styles, and genres with open arms.

The dialectics of 'change' is an essential part of the journey. New sounds, rhythms, and vibrations are all there waiting for exploration. Be open to failure and criticism and know that every stumble is a step forward on the path to enlightenment.

Ultimately, the practice of building beats with Buddhism is not just about making music: it is also about cultivating a lifestyle and mindset that champions inner harmony, dialogue with one's surroundings, and continual growth. Your music, like your life, is a divine journey that stretches towards an indefinite horizon, filled with possibilities only limited by your imagination.

Chapter 4. Exploring the Path of Audio Enlightenment

The domain of auditory enlightenment is a meticulous blend of cultivating the right mindset and the practical auditory skills. It delves into the wisdom of the Buddha and how his teachings can enhance and guide music production ventures.

4.1. Understanding Auditory Enlightenment

Auditory enlightenment brings together the realms of sonic perception with heightened awareness. In the context of electronic music production, achieving enlightenment means creating not just music, but a profound experience that echoes within the soul of the listener. The Buddha's teaching distinguished between 'right' and 'wrong' listening, and stressed the importance of active and deliberate attention. By applying mindfulness to the listening experience, we can absorb and interpret sounds more accurately and deeply.

In the sphere of electronic music, auditory enlightenment implicates the calibration of perception and skill—tuning our ears to discern the subtle layers of music production while resonating with the rhythm and pulse of the sounds.

4.2. The Sound of Silence

The Buddha emphasized the significance of silence. The world of electronic music, filled with beats, bleeps, and synth sweeps, might seem worlds away from the quietude of Buddhist philosophy. However, in the midst of these elaborate sonic constructions, the silence holds an equally important place. It creates breathing room within the tracks, allowing each sound effect to flourish and the listener to process and interpret.

Understanding silence isn't about muting the sounds but about manipulating the noise floor, giving each tone its space, and managing the frequency spectrum.

4.3. Mindfulness in Music Production

Mindfulness is an integral part of the Buddha's teachings, drawn from the core concept of being present in the moment. While creating music, being fully immersed can make the difference between a regular compilation and a sonic journey. Paying attention to every detail, understanding the intricacy of different sound waves, listening to the softest whisper of the synth, or the ringing echo of the drum beats can enhance the entire production process.

When immersing in the process of manipulating sounds, generating beats, and encoding emotions into electronic symphonies, mindfulness becomes paramount.

4.4. Mixing with Compassion

The Buddha's teaching of practicing compassion towards all beings can be leveraged into the production process as well. Treating each sound in production with respect, understanding its presence, contribution, and impact towards the entire soundscapes is indicative of a compassionate production approach.

A calm, compassionate outlook can produce better mixing decisions, enhancing the overall sonic cohesion and harmony of the track.

4.5. Finding Balance in Sound

In Buddhist philosophy, the Middle Way or the path of moderation between extremes is crucial. In the realm of electronic music, the Middle Way can resonate as finding the balance in our sounds. The balance should not only be between loudness and quietness but also in the diversity of tones, techniques, and elements used in the songwriting and production process.

By integrating the Middle Way with the practicalities of equalization, mastering, and compression, we can uphold the spirit of the teaching while creating enriched, dynamic musical pieces.

4.6. Communicating Emotions through Sound

The Buddha believed in the power of mindful speech or right communication. Extending this to music production involves creating a sonic language to communicate emotions effectively. Music, stripped to its essence, is a medium of conveying sentiments. Embracing this idea can transform the approach taken during the conception and composition stages, and guide the production towards a vibrant, more emotive result.

By playing with the interaction of different sound textures and dynamics, producers can 'speak volumes' without uttering a single word.

4.7. Auditory Enlightenment - A Continuous Journey

Enlightenment in the Buddha's teaching is not a destination, but a continuous process of self-discovery and growth. Similarly, the path of auditory enlightenment is also a journey, one requiring continuous refinement and development of one's craft and mindfulness.

As with any form of enlightenment, the path of auditory enlightenment is not an easy one. Yet, the rewards—aural masterpieces that resonate on a deeper emotional level—are plentiful. This confluence of soulful wisdom and technical acuity beckons, promising a transformative exploration into the depths of electronic music production.

Chapter 5. The Dharma of Digital Software: Choosing Your Tools Wisely

Just as a carpenter must choose his tools wisely, in the realm of electronic music production, the selection of your digital software is a foundational choice that will shape your creative journey. This chapter embraces the principles of the Buddha's teachings, known as Dharma, and applies them to the digital world, aiding you to navigate this fundamental choice with wisdom and clarity.

5.1. Mindful Consideration

Before embarking on the selection process, take time to sit in mindful consideration and self-reflection. This will allow you to explore what factors will matter the most. Ask yourself, what kind of music do you wish to create? How deep do you want to delve into the technical aspects of music production? What is your budget? What are your future aspirations? Practicing this self-reflection will ensure you choose the most beneficial digital audio workstation (DAW)—a tool that suits both your current and future needs.

5.2. Exploring the Landscape

A plethora of options awaits in the realm of DAWs. Some popular choices include Logic Pro, Pro Tools, Ableton Live, and FL Studio, each with its own set of strengths and nuances. You must explore each option and assess them based on their distinct characteristics. For instance, FL studio might be ideal for beat-makers due to its user-friendly sequencing capabilities. Ableton Live is praised for its loop-based approach, making it a compelling choice for live performances. Pro Tools excels in recording and precise editing, whereas Logic Pro offers an extensive range of virtual instruments.

5.3. Seek Guidance, Not Validation

As you delve deeper into the world of DAWs, you might find contrasting opinions and recommendations, which could turn overwhelming. While you must seek guidance and learn from others' experiences, remember to not be overly dependent on external advice. As Buddha said, "Do not look for a sanctuary in anyone except yourself." By all means, take recommendations, but your decision should resonate with your inner creative self.

5.4. Experimentation: The Path to Wisdom

Many DAWs offer trial versions of their software. Utilize these opportunities to explore the interface, workflow, and overall compatibility of each. Experiment, play around, and delve into the software's intricacies to learn if it aligns with your anticipated workflow. Remember, it's a journey. Don't rush. Recall the Buddha's teaching—"It is better to travel well than to arrive."

5.5. Economical Considerations

The choice of DAW should also reflect your budgetary considerations. Depending upon their feature set, complexity, and preferred user base, DAWs implement differing pricing models. Some stick to a one-time payment, while others have chosen the subscription-based model. It's essential to not just assess the upfront cost but the ongoing cost as well.

5.6. Hardware Integration

Whether you plan on predominantly using MIDI controllers or if you're heading towards a hardware-based sound design approach via synths, drum machines, or effects racks, the seamless integration of your DAW with hardware is of paramount importance. A DAW that communicates well with your gear not only simplifies the workflow but also opens up unrivalled creative potential.

5.7. Tap Into the Power of Communities

An active online community around a DAW can be an invaluable resource—offering tips, tutorials, plugins and patches, collective troubleshooting, inspirational projects, and even collaboration efforts. Communities reflect the liveliness of a DAW's ecosystem and are a strong testament to its continued development and resilience over time.

5.8. Tenets of Future-Proofing

In an ever-evolving digital world, change is the only constant. Choosing a DAW involves the subtle art of future-proofing—ensuring that your choice is adaptable and resilient to future shifts in the technological landscape. A DAW that continuously evolves, adapting to new formats, protocols, hardware, and exploits, future-proofs your creative endeavours.

By manifesting the principles of Dharma in choosing your digital software wisely, you embrace a path that is not only creatively fulfilling but fosters growth, learning, adaptability, and ultimately, liberation from the confines of technical limitations. In this harmonious marriage of music and mindfulness, remember, the tune of enlightenment reverberates beyond the strings of the instrument, reaching right from your DAW into the immense cosmos of expressive possibilities. Stay mindful, stay creative, stay enlightened.

Chapter 6. Nirvana in Noise: Navigating the World of Sound Design

Navigating the world of sound design, where the path to harmonic nirvana lies, requires exploratory instinct fueled by mindful insights. Herein, I attempt to deliver a profound understanding of this world— where synthesis intertwines with spirituality to create electronic artistry.

6.1. Embracing the Buddha's Mindfulness in Sound Design

Famous scriptures of Buddhism deliver the impactful message: "With our minds, we create the world." In the world of sound design, this timeless wisdom resonates deeply. When you sit in your studio, mindful of your thoughts and emotions, the world you create is influenced uniquely by these internal factors. Apply full consciousness to your creation, guiding each frequency and wave to unexpected heights.

When you create, the noise inside your head shouldn't be a distracting clamour; instead, it should reflect the serene realm of Buddha's teachings. This tranquillity enables you to listen more actively— to your inner self, the outside world, and the array of sounds your electronic tools can produce. Each hum, each vibration, and each rhythm, when given mindful attention, has the potential to build your sonic nirvana.

6.2. Awareness: Active Listening and Exploration

What does the chime of a bell sound like? How does the rustling of leaves sing to the wind? The heightened awareness from active listening, pivotal in teachings, can make a phenomenal difference to your sound design process. Create an inventory of sounds you discover in your solitude. From the melodious sigh of a breeze to the polyphony of a bustling marketplace, these sounds, once captured, become ingredients for your sonic recipe.

Explore your software and hardware capabilities; a synthesizer is like a Zen garden, where each module has a purpose, and every knob or fader adjustment transforms the landscape. Test the boundaries, and let your curiosity run wild. That buzzing transformer, the hum of a fluorescent light, or drones of a ceiling fan, all are opportunities for unique sound design. The world of noise can lead to nirvana if your awareness is fine-tuned.

6.3. The Middle Path: Balance in Sound Design

Buddha's teachings emphasize the middle path— equilibrium between extremes. Sound design mirrors this concept; it's an art that lies in balance. Frequencies need not combat for space; volume variabilities must be neither too high nor too low but just right. The ambience and reverb settings need to reflect a scene without overwhelming the core sounds. The equilibrium is what gives your sound design, depth and definition, just as teachings bring us inner peace and purpose.

6.4. The Four Noble Truths of Sound Design

Inspired by the Buddha's 'Four Noble Truths', we can evaluate a path for sound designers. The first truth, Dukkha, represents the dissatisfaction felt when a sound design does not resonate as hoped. The second, Samudaya, symbolizes that this dissonance arises from a lack of understanding of our tools or the message we wish to embody in our design.

The third truth, Nirodha, says that ceasing this discontent is possible. The fourth, Magga, underlines the correct method for accomplishing this harmony— continuing a careful exploration of your tools, seeking education, and practice. Like Buddhism's Noble Eightfold Path, our sound design challenges can be met—with right understanding, thought, speech, action, livelihood, effort, mindfulness, and concentration.

6.5. Elements of Sound Design: The Five Skandhas

In Buddha's teachings, the five skandhas explain the process of perception. These are form, sensation, perception, mental formations, and consciousness, each indispensable in the way we understand the world.

Relating this to sound design, form can regard the raw and foundational elements. This includes the frequencies, waveforms and our sonic palette. Sensation, it can be seen as the immediate reaction we have when encountering a sound. Perception stands as our understanding of it, categorising it as soothing, harsh, low, high, etc.

Mental formations are our thoughts, feelings and emotions evoked by the sound, the stories that arise in our minds. Consciousness is the overall comprehension of the sound as we perceive it as part of a larger whole, injecting it with personal and subjective meaning.

6.6. Apply The Buddha's Mindfulness into Your Sound Design Process

When you honour each sound, imbue your purpose into every note, and unleash your creativity harmoniously with the wisdom Buddha offers, you'll find yourself not just designing, but crafting masterpieces. You will unfold potential in the myriad depths of electronic music production. So breathe deeply, perceive actively, listen attentively, embrace calmness, and let the teachings become intrinsic to your creative process. It is here where we find nirvana in the noise, where mindfulness and music entwine to create a world of harmony and rhythm.

Chapter 7. Echos from Emptiness: The Art of Layering in Electronic Music

Electronic production, particularly layering, gifts us with profound lessons in harmony, complexity, and balance. It parallels the ebb and flow of emptiness and fullness, reinforcing the timeless teachings of Buddha.

7.1. Understanding the Basics of Layering

Layering is the art of combining different electronic sounds to create a visceral auditory experience that penetrates the listener's consciousness, reaching beyond simple melody and rhythm. It's akin to an artist mixing various pigments to bring a canvas to life, or a sculptor crafting from multiple materials to reveal a hidden form. Just as Buddha preached the art of harmony in our lives, layering allows us to create harmony between different electronic elements, creating a balanced and satisfying auditory experience.

A vital component of successful layering revolves around comprehending three essential aspects: frequency range, stereo field, and dynamics. Miss a beat in any of these, and your tracks may sound discordant, muddled, or improperly balanced.

1. **Frequency Range:** As Buddha taught, understanding the Self, or the essence, is crucial. Similarly, each sound has a fundamental frequency, its 'essence.' When layering, ensure that no two sounds compete in the same frequency range, thereby creating distraction and discordance.

2. **Stereo Field:** Stereo width elucidates the soundscape's expanse.

By suitably placing sounds in both stereo and mono, you can bring depth and spatial perception to your mixes, similar to bringing clarity to one's thought process while meditating.

3. **Dynamics:** This pertains to the volume fluctuation of a sound. By fluidly controlling the sound's dynamics, we can control its impact upon listeners, akin to controlling our mind's dynamics for a peaceful life.

7.2. Choosing the Right Sounds

Buddha taught about being attentive and selective with our thoughts and actions. The same goes for our choice of sounds. A prudent selection of sounds forms the cornerstone of an impactful layering.

By selecting sounds that complement each other, you empower them to work harmoniously, much like Buddha teachings on the importance of unity in achieving peace. When choosing sounds, remember that they should fit hand in glove in terms of frequency, stereo field, and dynamics.

1. **Identity:** Each sound should have a unique identity and purpose. There should be a rhythm, a melody, an essence. These are like the unique life paths Buddha advises we each must walk.

2. **Variety and Texture:** Just like life, music is replete with color and contrast. A little high-frequency sparkle here, some deep bass there, a sweeping synth pad adding texture – variety enhances the auditory journey.

3. **Synergy:** Synergy is the aesthetic principle at the heart of any great musical mix. Like the interdependence taught in Buddhism's teaching of Pratitya-samutpada, each layer in a track should be selected for how it sounds in conjunction with the others.

7.3. Techniques for Perfect Layering

Layering, like mindfulness, is a skill that improves with practice. The following techniques will help you slowly, but surely, master the art.

1. **Gain Staging and Balance:** An essential first step in layering. Each sound should be given its due space and importance, much like how Buddha advises us to balance our lives. Balance the sounds, and the majority of your work is done.

2. **EQ and Frequency Sidechaining:** Use EQ strategically to cut and boost frequencies, creating space for each sound. This is like the practice of mindful meditation where you recognize and command your plethora of thoughts, deciding which ones to entertain.

3. **Stereo Imaging:** Techniques like panning and delay can help place sounds in the stereo field, creating an expansive mixture of sounds that resonates with listeners.

4. **Dynamics Processing:** This includes compression, gating, and transient shaping, that help control the dynamics of the audio, much akin to controlling our mental states as Buddha advised.

7.4. Mixing with Inner Peace

Creating tranquil music requires a tranquil mind. It is here that the principles of Buddhism truly intermingle with the creative process.

1. **Mindful Listening:** Practice mindful listening to cultivate an ever-keen ear for subtleties in your mix. Each sound is a thought. Listen, understand, and then respond.

2. **Patience and Persistence:** Good layering comes with practice, experiment, and failure. Embrace these aspects and approach production with the same patience and persistence that Buddha preached in attaining enlightenment.

3. **Harmony:** Buddha preached harmony within oneself and with the universe. Strive for this harmony in your mix. All should be balanced, yet diverse, individual but interconnected.

7.5. Conclusions

Layering in electronic music production fulfills the versatile and inventive sonic vision that aligns with the spiritual teachings of Buddha. By thoughtfully weaving together the intricate elements of sound, tone, and rhythm, producers can embark on a transformative journey that illuminates their creative paths, much like Buddha's teachings enlighten our journey of life.

The Art of Layering in electronic music is a dive into emptiness, a dance with space, a journey that echoes the truth of Buddha's teachings – harmony, mindfulness, and patience. May your journey of layering be as enchanting and enlightening as your journey on Buddha's divine path.

Chapter 8. Melodies in Meditation: Harnessing Inner Peace for Creative Inspiration

Harnessing your inner peace for creative inspiration is an apt approach to create melodies that resonate with mindfulness. We'll embark on this journey in the following two-pronged approach – nurturing inner peace and directing that into creative inspiration.

8.1. Nurturing Inner Peace

We begin our journey with the cultivation of inner peace. This is a pivotal step as it forms the core from which your creative energy and inspiration will spring forth.

Buddhism emphasizes the practice of mindfulness and meditation as the path to achieving inner peace. To incorporate this into our composition process, let us begin with the practice of *anapanasati*, or mindfulness of breathing.

Stay with the breath, ignoring outer distractions.

As you delve deeper into the practice, you will start to find a unique rhythm emerging from your breath. This pulsating life force can serve as the undercurrent of your compositions – the grounding beats around which your melodies can weave and dance.

Over time, enhance your meditation routine. Introduce the concept of *metta*, or loving-kindness, radiating positivity towards yourself and all beings. Visualize the emotions and sensations as radiant light, with its ebbs and surges fostering textures for your melodies to explore.

8.2. Channeling Inner Peace into Creative Inspiration

Having established a routine for nurturing inner peace, the next stage is to funnel this tranquility into the essence of your melodies. This transition, when done mindfully, can embody depictions of your calmness and reflective state in your compositions.

Thinking of each melody as a 'sound-painting' of your emotions can be particularly powerful. On this note, the practice of *Vipassana*, or clear insight, can be valuable. It involves observing one's thoughts and emotions objectively, without judgement, and gaining a deeper understanding of oneself and the world around.

Transform these observations into musical ideas, leveraging this raw, emotional material in your melody creation.

Translate these 'sound-paintings' into ripe sources of inspiration for your electronic music compositions. Use them as a guide to infuse harmonies and progressions mirroring the intricacy, complexity, and intensity of your observed emotions.

8.3. From Synapses to Synthesizers

While meditation and mindfulness form the backbone, their incorporation into your physical set-up moves our theoretical discussion into the practical realm.

Creating a conducive work environment, your 'sonic temple,' aids in maintaining your inner peace during the creation process.

Synthesizers and DAWs: Choose hardware and software that you find intuitive and inspiring.

Your synthesizer is your tool for manipulating the raw emotions into electronic sounds. Use additive synthesis to reflect the multi-layered nature of your emotional spectrum, subtractive synthesis to mirror the negation of unnecessary mental clutter, FM synthesis to represent complex emotional interactions, and granular synthesis to mirror the fragmentation of thoughts and feelings.

As you journey along this path, don't forget to remain mindful throughout the entire process. Embrace the beautiful, challenging, and mystifying facets of creating electronic music as part of your meditative practice, with every note and every beat serving as an extension of your inner tranquility and emotional depth.

8.4. Finely Tuned Frequencies: Mastering the Art of Sonic Meditation

To close the loop in our quest for harnessing inner peace for creative inspiration, we must discuss the practice of sonic meditation. This centers around listening deeply and mindfully to our compositions, akin to how we listen to our thoughts during meditation.

As you listen, dissect your melodies, break them down into their constituent sounds and frequencies. Visualize these sounds shaping and forming patterns, resonating with your inner peace and emotions.

Remember to be patient with yourself and with the process. The path to mastery is often long and can come with frustration. However, an enlightened producer understands that frustration and setbacks are not obstacles, but necessary steps on the path to self-improvement and skill-enhancement.

8.5. Conclusion

The practice of utilizing inner peace for creative inspiration embodies the essence of mindfulness. It is a journey, not a destination. As you meditate, create, and listen, you continually cultivate mindfulness, achieving inner peace and creating melodies that reverberate with that tranquillity.

Remember, your pursuit of electronic music production should not exist separately from your spiritual practices but should rather serve as an extension. Therefore, let each chord resonate with your inner peace, every rhythm echo your heartbeat's rhythm, every note be an expression of your thoughts and feelings.

Harness this mindful approach to melodies, and you'll not only elevate your music but also your understanding and awareness of your inner self and the world around you. The resulting harmony of your electronic music will thus transcend sonic boundaries, creating sounds that truly resonate with the heart and soul.

Embrace the serenity that this journey brings. Relish every melody borne out of tranquillity and every note suffused with inner peace. Let your music serve as your spiritual guide, leading you further along the path of mindfulness, understanding, and, ultimately, a profound inner peace. By bridging the ancient wisdom of meditation with the modern practices of electronic music production, you can shape a transcendental auditory experience that embraces and celebrates the symbiosis of inner peace and creative inspiration.

Chapter 9. Karma in Composition: The Cyclic Nature of Music Creation

The concept of Karma, rooted in ancient Buddhist philosophy, suggests a paradox of determinism and freedom. It embodies the cyclic nature of cause and effect – every action, every thought, gives rise to a consequence that in turn shapes our future. And so, it is with music. Notes enthralling as they rise and fall all hinge on previous notes. Music ebbs and flows in cyclic rhythms just like life itself, continually defining and being defined by its progression. Let's explore this profound connection in detail.

9.1. Understanding Karma in Musical Terminology

Before embarking on the cyclical exploration of music, it's imperative to understand Karma in a musical context. Karma is the law of causality. In music, it refers to how melodies are generated from a small set of musical motives or collections of notes, as the decisions we make regarding composition impact the rest of the musical piece. Harmony, rhythm, and dynamics, they all resonate with the vibrancy of karma, the cyclic nature of patterns and variations shaping the rhythmic tide of our compositions.

9.2. Karma in Harmony

Harmony in music is not an isolated entity but a relational concept. It signifies how individual notes relate to each other over time, creating a coherent and pleasing sound. Achingly poignant chords, a dissonant note resolving to a consonant one, give a sense of karma –

the cycle of tension and release. By mindfully crafting the harmonic structure, you can breathe life into your composition and imbue it with an emotive essence.

9.3. Rhythm & Karma

Every beat in a musical piece counts, and together they drive the overarching rhythm - the pulse of music. The cyclic nature of rhythm, the rise and fall, acceleration, and deceleration, all mirror the universal phenomena of karma. The rhythmic patterns you choose govern the energy flow within your composition. A well-structured rhythm can evoke profound emotions, echo the karmic connection, and truly resonate with the listener.

9.4. Dynamics & Karma

The ebb and flow of music are molded by the dynamics, the variations in loudness between notes or phrases. From dramatic crescendos to subtle pianissimos, these dynamics infuse music with an infinite spectrum of feelings. This dynamism resembles Karma in real life, reflecting the fluctuations we experience in life's journey.

9.5. The Butterfly Effect in Music

The Butterfly Effect, a concept derived from chaos theory, speaks of interconnectivity, emphasizing that smallest changes can have significant impacts. This principle is profoundly etched in music creation. A single note alteration, a slight rhythmic modification, can transform your musical landscape. Thus, mindful decision-making at every step is essential.

9.6. Empathy in Creation

Empathy, the capacity to understand others' feelings, plays a crucial role in music creation. Through your composition, you can express shared emotions, enabling a sense of comfort or companionship, encouraging the listener to engage more deeply. In tune with the philosophy of karma, the love and understanding embedded in your music will reverberate back to you, in the form of appreciation and connection with your audience.

9.7. Applying Karma: Intentionality in Music Production

In music, as in life, every choice has a consequence. Intentionality refers to purposeful actions; in music production, it becomes a crucial element. When you approach your composition with clear intent, every note, every rhythm, every harmonic progression becomes a purposeful karmic journey. This mindfulness can transform your creation, rendering it not just a melodious tune but a story brimming with meaning and complexities.

9.8. Mindfulness in Practice

Realizing the influence of Karma in music creation is incomplete without inculcating mindfulness. By being present, being aware of the choices you make and how they shape your music, you can create a composition that not only sounds good but feels real and poignant. The karmic impact of mindfulness can transmute every note into a vibrant rhapsody.

Music creation is a continuous journey, marked by an intricate interplay of cause and effect. Understanding and implementing the lessons of Karma can lend a profound depth to your compositions, infusing them with a holistic sense of balance and meaning. Be mindful of the karmic cycles you start with each note and let your music reverberate with the universal essence of rhythm and harmony.

Chapter 10. Mastering with Mindfulness: Finishing Your Tracks with Serenity

The finale of your sonic creation journey comes with the practice of mastering, which is often considered technical and intricate. However, by using the principles of mindfulness and serenity, it can become another step in your path of sonic enlightenment, a meditative closure to the process of your musical creation.

10.1. The Harmony of Focus and Openness

One principle of mindfulness, as taught by Gautama Buddha, is the balanced co-adaptation of focus and openness. This applies here in the mastering stage. You must have singular focus on identifying and rectifying specific tone or level issues, however, you must also have openness to receive the overall feel and impression of the track.

The task can be achieved by initial assessments and fixes done in broad strokes, gently nudging the frequency spectrum and assessing how it affects overall feel of the song. After these primary assessments, you can dive deeper into intricate details, fixing specific issues that might be disrupting the harmonic balance.

10.2. Using Visualizations as Guides

Visualization plays a key in mastering, and it's here that the power of computer-based Digital Audio Workstations (DAWs) shines. While Waveforms and Spectrogram visual representations can provide critical insights, they shouldn't overshadow the aural experience.

Relying too much on visuals is equivalent to clinging, which Buddha warned against. By striking a balance between these visual aids and your own intuition and auditory judgment, you foster a sense of equilibrium.

10.3. The Rule of Non-attachment

Non-attachment is at the very heart of Buddha's teachings. When it comes to mastering, the principle of non-attachment implies we must assess every mix objectively without the biases of emotional or physical fatigue. If you listen to the track repeatedly while mixing, you become attached to certain elements that may not serve the collective harmony of the track. Remember, mastering is akin to adding the final seasoning to the meal: it should embellish the track, not overpower it.

One practical way to apply non-attachment is by providing adequate rests between mixing and mastering. This temporal separation aids in achieving a fresh and objective response to the mix.

10.4. Meditate with Metering

Mastering is a subtle art. It's about fine-tuning rather than drastic alterations, requiring a vigilant and meditative mindset. Metering plays a fundamental role in achieving this subtlety. On a practical level, it includes monitoring volume levels to achieve loudness, while being mindful of the dynamics.

Loudness Wars have posed a chasm in the music industry, prompting the production of louder music often at the expense of dynamic range. Buddha's Middle Way principle invites us to steer clear of extremities and seek balance. In the context of mastering, loudness should be sufficient to achieve clarity and impact, but not so much that it inhibits dynamics and fatigues the listener.

10.5. The Silence Between the Notes

Buddha shared, "The heart of the path is quite easy. There's no need to explain anything at length. Let go of love and hate and let things be. That is all that I teach." The same ideology can be applied in mastering.

While it's necessary to have detailed engagement with technicalities, at times, the unadulterated enjoyment of music can get lost in the process. Shying away from preset notions, one must perceive the gaps, the absence, the silence, in music. It's within these gaps that music breathes, resounds, and achieves depth. Appreciating these spaces adds to the final soulful touch in mastering.

10.6. The Sound of Serenity: Inner Peace Reflects Outward

Mastering, in essence, is about sealing the harmonious integrity of musical elements. Serenity, an integral part of Buddha's teachings, in this context means a peaceful state of mind that isn't easily disturbed by unexpected challenges.

As you master, strive to maintain this serenity even with inevitable tweaks and fixes. Remember, music is a reflection of your inner state. The peace, calm, and serenity that you harbor within will reverberate through your music, touching listeners deeply.

There can be no end to musical learning, much similar to the lifelong journey towards enlightenment as Buddha taught. As you follow this serenely jubilant path of music production, may you continue to create soulful, resonating masterpieces guided by inner peace and mindfulness. Embrace the Buddha's wisdom as your unseen guide, and let the rhythmic harmony resonate within and beyond.

Chapter 11. The Bodhisattva Beat: Giving Life to Your Electronic Music

Creating music is not just mixing audios or creating beats; it is a profound journey into the depths of one's soul, seeking undiscovered melodies that resonate with the universe. The practice of a Bodhisattva – a being committed to attaining Buddhahood – mirrors this exploration. They willingly plunge into the realm of Dukkha (suffering, unease) to understand and transcend it. In this chapter, we will align this spiritual endeavor with your sonic experiments in electronic music production.

11.1. The Harmonic Nexus: Understanding Your Intent

In Buddhist philosophy, everything begins with intention. Before we even tap our first note or adjust a level on the mixing desk, we must delve into the core intention behind making music. Ask yourself, what am I attempting to manifest with this track? Is the objective merely to incite movement, or is there an emotional, intellectual or spiritual voyage I want to embark my audience on? Every note we select and every waveform we shape should resonate with our intention. This alignment births harmony within the track and fosters an intimate dialogue between the music and the listener.

11.2. The Eightfold Path: A Producer's Perspective

Just as Buddha outlined the eightfold path towards enlightenment, let's present an eight-step pathway towards creating mindful, spiritually-imbued electronic music.

1. Right Understanding: Understand the tools at your disposal profoundly. Dive into the inner workings of your DAW (Digital Audio Workstation), your physical and virtual instruments, your effect chains, and more.

2. Right Intent: As established earlier, begin each track with a well-defined intent.

3. Right Speech: Essentially the language of your music. Be conscious of the vocabularies of sound you are using and how they communicate your intent.

4. Right Action: Every act in the creation process should align with your understanding and intent, from the selection of sounds to their arrangement in the track.

5. Right Living: Create an environment that fosters creativity and spiritual alignment. This includes the physical space of your studio as well as the mental space within which you create.

6. Right Effort: Music creation is often a bi-play of inspiration and effort. Balancing these two forces can ensure a smooth and harmonious process.

7. Right Mindfulness: Stay present at every moment of the production. Whether you're adjusting a knob or crafting a complex polyrhythm, be fully there.

8. Right Concentration: Channel your full focus into creating. This doesn't mean cutting off the exterior world completely, but understanding when to draw borders and when to break them.

11.3. Sculpting Soundscapes with the Middle Way

The Buddha preached 'The Middle Way' as a path of moderation. Balance is everything. In electronic music, this balance is crucial in various areas. The first and most apparent is the auditory balance. Too much or too little of certain frequencies can obscure your track's central message, leading to a sonic imbalance. The 'Middle Way' philosophy asks you to be attentive to EQs, levels, stereo field, and the overall tonal structure of your composition.

Besides, 'The Middle Way' is also about balancing silence and sound. Buddha once said, "Better than a thousand hollow words, is one word that brings peace." This wisdom applies to the realm of sound too. Strive to integrate the tranquility of silence with the vibrancy of your beats. Let your music breathe, allow space for the listener's emotion to step into the track and echo the essence of your intent.

11.4. The Four Noble Truths of Electronic Music Production

The Four Noble Truths lay the foundation of all Buddhist teachings, highlighting the nature of suffering and the way towards liberation. Transforming them into the context of music production, we can discern intriguing insights:

1. The Truth of Mutable Audio (Anicca): Just as all things in life are transient and subject to change, so are our tracks. Sounds can be manipulated and transformed in innumerable ways. The key lies in embracing this mutability and utilizing it to shape aurally-pleasing experiences.

2. The Truth of Unsatisfactory Sound (Dukkha): Not every sonic experimentation will give us the desired result. But it's important to understand that dissatisfaction can catalyze exploration and eventually lead to paths of unique, stunning soundscapes.

3. The Truth of the Causation of Unsatisfactory Sound (Samudaya): The more we learn about the causes of 'unsatisfactory sound,' the more skilled we become at avoiding or addressing these pitfalls.

4. The Truth of the Path to Satisfactory Sound (Magga): This path is

nothing but a combination of creativity, technical skill, mindfulness, and relentless curiosity.

11.5. From Dukkha (Suffering) to Sukha (Pleasure): Production Challenges and Triumphs

Every creative process has its ebbs and flows. There will be moments of frustration when a melody doesn't quite hit the mark or a mix feels muddled. Don't perceive these hurdles as deterrents; instead, view them as opportunities to understand better and navigate your sonic landscape, to weave intricacies that push your creative boundaries.

Breathe in patience and breathe out perseverance. The musical universe is a vast expanse teeming with countless undiscovered sonic galaxies. Enjoy this journey of serendipitous explorations and profound revelations; know that the path should be as gratifying as the destination. As Buddha said, "It is better to travel well than to arrive." Your sonic journey is unique to you. Embrace every note, every beat, every pause, and every resonance, for therein lies the essence of mindful creation.

In this beautiful intertwining of spiritual wisdom and electronic music production, you birth an omnipresent resonance. A resonance that bridges the earthly and digital, balances the physical and the ethereal, and creates soundscapes that are not just heard but felt. This is the birth of the Bodhisattva Beat in your electronic music.

Remember, as of a Bodhisattva, your purpose is to explore, understand, learn, and transcend, bringing harmony not just to your music but to the hearts of your listeners. It is they who dance to your music, they who feel your beats seep into their veins and spirits. You're shaping more than mere sound. You're shaping experiences, moments, emotions, and memories. That is the true essence and the divine power of the Bodhisattva Beat.